The Dirty Thirties:

A History of the Dust Bowl

By Howard Brinkley

BookCaps™ Study Guides
www.bookcaps.com

© 2012. All Rights Reserved.

Table of Contents

ABOUT HISTORYCAPS 3

INTRODUCTION 4

CHAPTER 1: CAUSES 5

    THE GREAT PLOW-UP 6
    DROUGHT 8
    THE STORMS 9
    BLACK SUNDAY 14

CHAPTER 2: HUMAN DISPLACEMENT 18

    ROUTE 66 25

CHAPTER 3: GOVERNMENT RESPONSE 28

    RESETTLEMENT ADMINISTRATION 30
    THE PLOW THAT BROKE THE PLAINS 31
    MIGRANT CAMPS 34
    FARM SECURITY ADMINISTRATION (FSA) 36
    MIGRANT MOTHER 40
    FLEEING THE DUST BOWL 42

CHAPTER 4: THE DUST BOWL IN POPULAR CULTURE 44

    THE GRAPES OF WRATH 44
    WOODY GUTHRIE 47

CHAPTER 5: LONG-TERM EFFECTS OF THE DUST BOWL 51

CONCLUSION 54

About HistoryCaps

HistoryCaps is an imprint of BookCaps™ Study Guides. With each book, a brief period of history is recapped. We publish a wide array of topics (from baseball and music to science and philosophy), so check our growing catalogue regularly (**www.bookcaps.com**) to see our newest books.

Introduction

The Dust Bowl was the largest ecological disaster in United States history, coinciding with the nation's worst economic crisis, the Great Depression of the 1930s. Massive dust storms, combined with nearly a decade of drought, wreaked havoc on parts of Colorado, New Mexico, Texas, Oklahoma, Kansas, Nebraska, and Arkansas. The storms were a relentless threat to the environment and the health and welfare of those in their path. The effects of the dust storms were far-reaching, impacting not just the farmers and their families, but the state of California. Many who were forced off their land viewed the state as a mecca and it became the new home for millions of former Midwesterners. However, many families stayed in the Great Plains and reluctantly turned to the federal government for assistance to make ends meet. The government's new role as a provider of economic relief and social aid was met with gratitude by some and anger by others.

Chapter 1: Causes

Following the end of World War I, America's farmers found themselves in the midst of an economic depression. The irony of the situation was that some of it was due to their own hard work because the more crops they produced, the lower the crop prices fell. Falling prices are good for consumers, but not for those who are producing the goods. Given that in the 1920s about 20 percent of Americans were farmers and just under half lived in rural areas, this impacted a large percentage of the nation.

Almost all farmers already made less money per year than the average laborer in manufacturing or industry. Millions of rural Americans were still without indoor plumbing or electricity. By 1918, prices for many crops plunged by as much as two-thirds, leaving farmers with less money to feed their families and pay down debts for their land or tractors, purchased on credit when times were better. However, one crop did hold its value: wheat. Between 1910 and 1917, the price for a bushel of wheat shot up from 80 cents to $2. Prices came down a bit after the war, but not as much as the price for crops such as corn or cotton.

Unfortunately for farmers, though, wheat prices steadily declined into the mid-1920s, yet farmers continued to plant more and more wheat. As the prices dropped, farmers believed they needed to plant more to allow them to sell more, but this vicious cycle only continued to drive prices down. In the 1920s, farmers produced 300 percent more wheat than the previous decade. Meanwhile, prices sunk to 75 cents per bushel.

Wheat farmers needed more land for all of these wheat crops. The railroad companies and the states, which published beautiful advertisements and brochures promising a bountiful harvest of the likes never seen before, lured Americans to the southern Plains. The untouched grasslands were portrayed as the answer to the prayers of farmers who only needed the tenacity and courage to turn the virgin territory into acre after acre of wheat.

The Great Plow-Up

Many of the farmers that descended on the Plains brought techniques that worked well for them in the Northeast. They also held the belief that if a team of horses could turn over three acres of ground a day, then a tractor was even better because it could handle up to 50 acres. These farmers were not prepared for the terrain of the Plains, though, and without realizing what they were doing, they were creating an environment that was ripe for disaster.

Before the farmers came with plows, the land was used by the earliest settlers for grazing for their livestock. Prior to that, Native American tribes roamed the grassland in search of buffalo. By plowing the land, the root system that used to hold the grass in place was gone, leaving very loose topsoil. When 1931 began, farmers of the Plains had no idea about the disaster that would soon come because they were experiencing record-breaking wheat crops. The federal government was not only not helping the problem, it was compounding it by encouraging the farmers to produce more and more wheat. The slogan was "Food Will Win the War." One propaganda poster said, "Wheat is needed for the allies. Waste nothing." The consensus was that if the U.S. was to be a dominant world power, it needed to produce like one. Ralph Watkins from the U.S. National Resources Planning Board said in 1942, "We will emerge from this struggle as the dominant power; dominant in naval power, dominant in air power, dominant in industrial capacity, dominant in mineral production, dominant in agricultural production. These are the basic resources of power."

The Great Plains is known for its cycles of rain followed by drought. Much of the area of the 150,000 square mile region of the panhandles of Oklahoma and Texas and parts of Kansas, Colorado, and New Mexico get very little rainfall at all. The soil is loose and winds can be ferocious, especially in areas where there are few trees to act as windbreaks. However, many farmers lived by the creed that "the rain will follow the plow." Except that didn't happen.

High winds are a part of life on the Plains, but many people did not notice when the winds began to bring in more dust. When the rains stopped in the summer of 1931, the wheat crops withered away and died. With nothing to protect the loose layer of topsoil, the howling winds blew away the dead wheat and the underlying dirt and carried it all away. What was once a wheat field became bare, hard ground in a matter of minutes.

Drought

Much of the United States experienced a drought in the 1930s, but it struck the Great Plains particularly hard. There were three significant waves of drought, coming in 1934, 1936, and 1939, although some areas of the Plains saw no significant rain for four - possibly up to eight - years. NASA scientists have been able to analyze climate data for the past 100 years and, using a computer model, determined the cause of the 1930s drought.

Most of the rain in the Great Plains falls in the spring and summer. Westerly trade winds that blow from the equator usually bring moisture westward up to the Plains from the Gulf of Mexico. However, warmer air over the Atlantic makes it less dense and more apt to rise. When this happens, cooler, high-pressure air moves east, carrying the moist air from the Gulf of Mexico with it. Temperatures in the Pacific Ocean were cooler than normal and temperatures in the Atlantic Ocean were warmer than normal. According to NASA, the unstable sea temperatures created the dry air and hot temperatures in the Plains for most of the decade.

The prairie grasslands, native to the region, are able to withstand drought conditions. However, wheat needs water to grow and the lack of rain not only killed the wheat crops, it made the soil extremely loose and dry. The dry soil meant that there was less evaporation, which compounded the already dry conditions. When the winds came, dust storms were created. The land was as dry as powder and simply blew away.

The Storms

With no significant rain for the past year, dust storms began to form by 1932. At first, they were an annoyance. The thick dust made it difficult to see and covered everything in dirt. School was cancelled because it was hard for kids to see clearly enough to get there and, like the inside of their houses, everything inside the schoolhouse was coated in dust. Eventually, with the storms becoming a daily occurrence, schools were kept open and children just did the best they could to get there.

As the black clouds intensified, some took to stuffing towels and rags in doorways and around windows to try and keep the dust at bay. As the winds got more ferocious and the air remained hot, some hung wet sheets on their porches at night to act as a primitive air conditioning system. By morning, the sheets would be caked in mud. Dirt would be piled near doorways like snowdrifts and be so deep that it was as high as the windowsills. To get out of the door, people needed to climb out the window and make their way through mounds of dirt just to get to the front door and start digging out. The dust was so thick inside the houses that shovels were needed to clear the floor.

In Boise City, Oklahoma, Hazel Lucas Shaw was just starting a family when the dust storms came and she kept a written record of her experiences in the Dust Bowl. She said that attempts to start a garden were futile due to the thick layers of dust that would fall onto her small plot of land. Like many, she watched as dust made its way through any cracks in the walls of her home and settled on bed linens, kitchen tables, and plates. When she woke up in the mornings, the only area around her that was not covered in dust was where her head had covered her pillow. Margie Daniels, who lived through the Dust Bowl as a young girl in Hooker, Oklahoma, said, "Everything was full of dust. If you were cooking a meal, you'd end up with dust in your food and you would feel it in your teeth. You'd start to eat and when you would drink water or something, you would bite down and you always felt like you had grit between your teeth."

As the storms persisted, simply surviving became the biggest challenge of all. When cattle that succumbed to the dust were slaughtered, their stomachs would be filled with the black dirt from the skies. People became sick with dust pneumonia as their respiratory systems battled for a clean breath of air, which was nearly impossible to find. Few plants or animals could survive, making finding sources of food very difficult. Despite all of this, the Department of Health initially denied that the dust was a health risk. It proclaimed that since the dust was coming from wide-open spaces with no disease, swallowing "sterile dirt" could harm no person of normal health.

The extremely dry air also created a tremendous amount of static electricity. The static electricity in the air meant that simply hugging someone or shaking hands could knock a person over. It caused cars to stall because the ignition systems shorted out and would not start again until to the storm passed. People started dragging chains and wires under their vehicles to keep them grounded. Many put cloth on doorknobs and oven knobs to prevent getting shocked. The simple act of using a water pump handle or grabbing a frying pan could lead to a jolt of electricity. Some people reported seeing flames shoot out of the shutoff wire of their windmills or blue sparks jump off of barbed-wire fences.

The electricity also killed crops and gardens. Melt White, a child in Dalhart, Texas during the Dust Bowl, recalled, "I had some little watermelons about as long as your little finger, just as pretty and shiny, a little fuzz on 'em, you know? And went out the next mornin' after one of them sand storms and there are the watermelons' vines whipped around and them little melons just black as tar. It was completely just because of static electricity and that continuous wind."

Some believed that if they could only make it rain, they could keep the dust at bay. In June 1934, prayer bands were organized throughout the state of Kansas to pray for rain. The state also saw a growth in salesmen selling any number of rainmaking devices to try to get the skies to open, although Kansans had been through that three decades before and did not have much faith in these machines, which failed them in the past. In July 1934 in Mitchell, South Dakota, when the temperatures soared over 100 degrees and got as high as 114, town residents dropped to their knees in prayer when they heard the noon church bells signaling to them that it was time to pray for rain. On August 8, President Franklin D. Roosevelt was deemed a "rainmaker" when his visits to two drought-stricken states were followed by rain.

One of the most well-know rainmakers was Tex Thornton, an oilman and an expert on the volatile explosive, nitroglycerin. Like many, including soldiers in World War I, Thornton believed that a properly placed explosion could result in the heavens opening up with rain. Dalhart was one of the small towns hit the hardest by the Dust Bowl. On June 27, 1931, with the temperature sitting at 112 degrees, the town bank closed. With the dust storms just beginning, hard times were ahead for Dalhart, which would endure a decade of bankruptcy and dust pneumonia.

Thornton arrived in town in 1935. He told the town's citizens that he could make it rain. For many days in a row, Thornton trudged out into the middle of dust and wind and blasted dynamite toward the sky. On the third day, people living in towns east of Dalhart, getting only clouds of dust and not rain, asked Thornton to stop the blasting. Blasting out in the fields until midnight, the noise kept most of Dalhart awake. After adjusting his approach by sending balloons of explosives into the clouds, there was a noticeable drop in temperature, followed by a dusting of snow. The next day, the snow turned to sleet as the temperature warmed up. It should be noted that it also snowed in Albuquerque, Denver, and Dodge City, Kansas, which was well out of Thornton's range. However, many in the Dalhart area thanked Thornton and some thought the drought was over. Of course, it was far from over and would continue through the end of the decade.

Black Sunday

Before Thornton made an effort at making it rain in Dalhart, the High Plains had been enduring dust storms for weeks throughout the spring of 1935. Many counties in Oklahoma, Texas, and Kansas did not see a day without dust for six straight weeks. The worst storm of them all came on April 14, when daylight turned darker than midnight due to a wall of black dust that descended on the land. The day started innocently, even pleasant for many people, many of whom took advantage of the sunny day to do chores or have a picnic after church. However, as the afternoon wore on, temperatures began to fall and there was a nervous energy in the air.

Suddenly, around 4 p.m. on the Oklahoma panhandle, an enormous black cloud formed out on the horizon and moved in quickly. It moved rapidly toward the south and the southeast across the state. The clouds brought with it cool temperatures and pushed a wall of black dust, sustained by winds of approximately 40 miles per hour. The Oklahoma and Texas panhandles bore the brunt of the storm, which resembled a tsunami, except the storm held dust, not water. By 5:15, the storm hit Boise City, Oklahoma and by 7:20, it made its way to Amarillo, Texas. The air was so thick with dust that people could not see their hands in front of their face. Avis D. Carlson wrote in the *New Republic,* "The impact is like a shovelful of fine sand flung against the face."

For those caught out in the storm, they had little choice but to try and find shelter to wait it out. Ed and Ada Phillips, along with their 6 year-old daughter, got caught in the massive wall of black dust near Boise City. They joined a group of other people who had discovered an abandoned two-room adobe hut and were trapped there for four hours. They were afraid if they left, they would suffocate.

The Amarillo newspaper reported that visibility was zero miles for 12 minutes. Pauline Winkler Grey wrote for the Kansas Historical Society:

> "Even the birds were helpless in the turbulent onslaught and dipped and dived without benefit of wings as the wind propelled them. As the wall of dust and sand struck our house the sun was instantly blotted out completely. Gravel particles clattered against the windows and pounded down on the roof. The floor shook with the impact of the wind, and the rafters creaked threateningly. We stood in our living room in pitch blackness."

When it finally ended, this single, massive dust storm had moved twice as much dirt and debris as the workers moved when digging the Panama Canal. With the help of winds of up to 60 miles per hour, 300 million tons of dry earth sailed across the Plains. Small wildlife was killed instantly. Larger animals suffocated within a few hours. People who could not find shelter had their lungs filled with dirt, their eyes blinded, and their skin sliced. A man in Kansas, who became disoriented while trying to drive home, drove off the road and was found the next day, smothered in dirt. It was this epic storm that sent many on the road to the West.

Chapter 2: Human Displacement

Americans in the 1930s were on the move. As often seems the case when times get tough, they were headed west. However, the migration toward the Pacific coast was not all attributed to Dust Bowl refugees. In fact, 75 percent of those who were hit by the drought and dust storms stayed in the Plains. The editor of the *Dalhart Texan,* John McCarty, started a group he called The Last Man's Club. Members had to sign a pledge that read, "In the absence of an act of God, serious family injury, or some other emergency, I pledge to stay here as the last man and to do everything I can to help other last men remain in this country. We promise to stay here `til hell freezes over and skate out on the ice."

The idea that hoards of white families from the Great Plains packed all of their belongings on wagons and joined the great migration to California during the Great Depression is not a completely accurate one. It is true that a large number of people from the Midwest moved to California during those years and it is also true that many of them were driven out by the Dust Bowl. However, it is important to keep in mind that the areas most affected by the Dust Bowl were small towns and counties with few residents. In comparison to the overall numbers of migrants, Dust Bowl refugees were far from the majority. Also, the image of wagons is a product of fiction. Nearly everyone had a car, which were made affordable by Henry Ford.

Those that come from the Midwest were largely from eastern Oklahoma, Texas, Arkansas, and Missouri. These were areas of the country that were impacted by the drought and the Great Depression, but not the Dust Bowl. While numbers are difficult to accurately calculate, historians estimate that anywhere between 300,000 and 400,000 people from these states moved to California. Of those, nearly 95 percent were white. There seemed to be an equal number of men and women and families tended to be large. Most were young.

At least half of the people who migrated to the West during this time were not farmers. Many had been working in manufacturing or some other type of blue collar job before they lost those jobs due to the Depression. They headed west to populate the cities of California, and, to a lesser degree, Arizona, and find work. Still, even if the popular image of Route 66 being clogged with displaced farmers and their families is somewhat skewed, it is that image that helped change public policy. Prior to 1941, states could restrict who crossed their borders. In many cases, they tried to prevent the poor from entering their state, which went hand-in-hand with strict vagrancy laws. To apply for public aid, people typically had to prove long-term residency. In 1936, the Los Angeles police department set up the "Bum Blockade". This border patrol was set up at major railroad and highway intersections to turn away anyone suspected of being a "bum." However, in 1941, the Supreme Court ruled in Edwards v. California that states did not have the authority to restrict migration by anyone, poor or not, across interstate borders.

Even if the Dust Bowl was not solely responsible for the migration west, the 1930s still saw the greatest mass migration in the nation's history with over 2.5 million people heading west from the Great Plains. By the time the 1930s ended, the only states with smaller populations than when the decade began were states in the Plains. Oklahoma lost over 18 percent of its 1930 population, accounting for over 440,000 people. Kansas saw a drop of 227,000 in its population over the decade. Twenty-three of the 32 counties in the Texas panhandle decreased in population. As many as 10,000 houses in the Plains were simply abandoned, many residents not even bothering to shut the door behind them.

Many of those who left did not go far. Some went on to the next town, next county, or next state. Of the 309,000 people who left Oklahoma between 1935 and 1940, 142,000 went to a neighboring state, such as Texas. One group of Texans migrated en masse to Western New Mexico and Mesa County, Colorado saw 500 families from Dust Bowl areas move in within a five-year period. Most who went farther than that kept going to the Western U.S. During the 1930s, the Pacific Northwest attracted 460,000 migrants and 25 percent of those came from the Northern Plains. Those who went there did not find much good farm land and either had to settle on abandoned land, apply for federal relief, or move on to the cities to find work.

While some migrants who left their general region stopped and made lives in New Mexico and Arizona, most headed for California. In one 15-month period, over 86,000 migrants poured over the California border, which was more than entered the state during the Gold Rush. By the end of the 1930s, California had a 20 percent increase in population, adding over one million new residents. What was it about California? For starters, the state had portrayed itself as a tropical paradise. The only thing many people from the Plains knew about California was what they saw in travel brochures or on posters, which was primarily palm trees, sunshine, and the ocean. It is true that the mild climate was an attraction for many. For farmers, a milder climate equated to a longer growing season and more diverse crops.

California also offered more employment opportunities that most other locations. Some people had trouble finding work, but most eventually found suitable jobs, particularly in Los Angeles and San Francisco. Others settled in the San Joaquin Valley, which includes Bakersfield, and worked in town or picked cotton or other crops. Relief from the government helped supplement income until jobs were more readily available in the 1940s, particularly when jobs in defense plants were open.

No matter where migrant workers came from, in California they were all considered "Okies." The term was not meant kindly and at one theater in the San Joaquin Valley, a sign read, "Negroes and Okies Upstairs." Some Californians viewed Okies as somehow inferior to the rest of Americans. Satirist and writer H.L. Mencken said of poor rural Americans, "They are simply, by God's inscrutable will, inferior men and inferior they will remain until, by a stupendous miracle, He gives them equality among His angels. Mencken went so far as to suggest that they be sterilized to prevent breeding. Most Californians did not go that far in their bigoted beliefs, assuming that the migrants had been displaced by a natural disaster, but many did not appreciate the presence of the transplanted people from the Plains.

Large commercial growers were happy to have the migrants, though, since immigration restrictions in 1929 had cut off their supply of inexpensive labor from Mexico. Farmers from the Plains that expected to own a plot of land quickly discovered that commercial growers had what amounted to a monopoly on the cropland. The landowners needed workers to harvest crops including peaches, prunes, lettuce, oranges, lemons, cotton, and flax. Most workers started in Brawley in the Imperial Valley and made their way up to Santa Barbara, the Central Valley, and then they continued north to Washington. These migrant workers simply went where the work was. The growers provided crude camps for the migrant workers, but with only three state inspectors responsible for monitoring over 8,000 camps, the conditions were uncomfortable and unsanitary.

The effect of having so many workers available to work in the fields was a reduction in wages. There were only about 175,000 jobs available at the peak of the growing season, with twice as many people wanting the jobs. Migrants could work about half the year and made around $350 for their work, which was half of what the California Relief Administration considered appropriate for meeting basic needs. The migrants had little choice, though, if they wanted to work in the fields. Attempts to organize where met with violence and there was always a new batch of workers waiting, often literally alongside the road.

Those who could not find work set up "ditchback" camps along the irrigation ditches, sometimes called "Little Oklahomas." Often, even with whole families working in the fields, they did not make enough money to support themselves and set up camp along the ditches. With no electricity, running water, or toilet facilities, none of the camps were suitable for human living, but the camps near Imperial Valley were considered the worst. Relief workers discovered a family of 10 people living out of a 1921 Ford. The mother was suffering from tuberculosis and pellagra, a condition brought on by vitamin deficiency, but she had made an effort to set up a home amid the filth. She set up a "kitchen" using boxes for a cupboard, a rusty can as a pot, and water from the irrigation ditch for laundry. The ditch also served as their toilet. When told that her family would have to leave, the woman said flatly, "I wonder where we can go."

Route 66

Most who did flee the Dust Bowl en route to California traveled on the famed highway, Route 66. It was nicknamed "The Mother Road" by John Steinbeck in his classic work of fiction about a Dust Bowl family, "The Grapes of Wrath." It stretched 2,400 miles between Chicago and Los Angeles, making its way through eight states. One of the towns that migrants passed through was Flagstaff, Arizona, in the northern part of the state. Florence Hanan Currier, was a resident of Flagstaff when displaced families passed through town. "It was sad to see families on the move and in need. We lived in a small trailer and parked in Kit Carson Forestry camp. While there we saw and talked to many families who had left the Dust Bowl areas, many striving to find a better life."

About 65 percent of the nation's westbound traffic took Route 66 in the 1930s. There were very few hotels available, so most people camped along the way. Diners, gas stations, and campgrounds were kept busy with the traffic and, since Route 66 passed through small towns, the people displaced by the Depression helped to keep the small towns thriving. Cars were affordable for most farmers, but they broke down consistently along Route 66, which was not completely paved until 1937. It was not uncommon to see families waiting by the side of the road for tires to be patched or radiators to be filled with water. One of the families that migrated west on Route 66 was the Haggard family, who would have a son, Merle, who became a country singing legend. Flossie Haggard said the trip from Oklahoma to California went well until their car broke down in the Arizona desert. She recalled:

> We were out of water, and just when I thought we weren't going to make it, I saw this boy coming down the highway on his bicycle. He was going all the way from Kentucky to Fresno. He shared a quart of water with us and helped us fix the car. Everybody'd been treating us like trash and I told this boy, "I'm glad to see there's still some decent folks left in this world.

Others broke down along the way and had to wait until they made enough money to continue their journey. Some intentionally planned to go as far as Arizona, make money picking cotton, then move on. Marvin Montgomery's family tried to make it in a 1929 Hudson that was burning oil and gas, forcing them into a five-week layover in Arizona. Parents of another country singer, Buck Owens, had to stop in Mesa, Arizona, but didn't leave for another 14 years.

Chapter 3: Government Response

In many ways, it was the federal government that created the Dust Bowl. While most agree that overfarming the land and poor soil management is largely to blame for the disaster, it was the government that set the wheels in motion with the Homestead Act. After the Civil War, the government wanted to accelerate westward expansion and encouraged Americans to move to the Plains by offering 160 acres of government-surveyed land for a small filing fee. After five years of living on the land, it was owned outright. While it seemed like a good deal, this led to a boom in small farms. Between 1880 and 1920, hundreds of thousands of small acre farms popped up in the Plains states. By the 1930s, two-thirds of American farms on the Great Plains were less than 500 acres, compared to 40 percent by 1978.

Small farms operated differently than large farms. In order to make ends meet, the farmers worked the land more aggressively. Soil conservation was virtually unknown, and, considering that Americans did not know what the Native Americans understood about the land, neither the government nor the new occupants of the land was prepared for the inevitable time of drought. Small wheat farms would produce when there was rain, but they were doomed to fail when the rains did not come. Therefore, one of the first orders of business for the federal government was to abolish homesteading, which it did in 1934.

Shortly after Franklin Roosevelt took office in 1933, he appointed Henry Wallace as the Secretary of Agriculture. In 1933, Wallace wrote the Agricultural Adjustment Administration (AAA), which was approved by Congress. The AAA Act paid farmers to stop producing certain crops such as wheat, cotton, tobacco, corn, and rice, as well as slaughter their hogs. The intent was to reduce supply, increase demand, and help put money directly into the farmers' pockets. Despite the resistance of many farmers, who did not want to be viewed as accepting charity, most had no choice but to participate in AAA. Without it, they would have starved or been forced to abandon their farms.

However, in 1936, the Supreme Court ruled that the AAA Act was unconstitutional. Money for the farmers had been coming from a tax levied on the manufacturers that used the products that the farmers produced. The Supreme Court said that the manufacturers could not be legally obligated to pay the farmers and participate in a production control program.

In 1938, the second phase of the AAA program was rolled out in the form of the Soil Conservation and Domestic Allotment Act. Instead of being paid for not producing crops, farmers were paid for not planting crops that depleted the soil and for planting crops that preserved the soil such as grasses, legumes, and crops that could be used for feed. This worked more to the benefit of the farmers because any part of their land that was used according to the AAA guidelines was eligible for payment. There were critics of the program, particularly among the large grain dealers, but overall, the funding was a significant source of income for farmers between 1933 and 1937. In 1934, farmers in Baca County, Colorado received checks totaling over $190,000. By the end of that year, counties in the Texas panhandle received over $7.5 million in AAA payments.

Resettlement Administration

In 1935, President Roosevelt created the Resettlement Administration (RA), which encompassed other programs that Roosevelt had developed to assist the poor. The RA's central goal was to assist those hit by the economic crisis in rural communities. Rexford Tugwell was named the head of the program. Tugwell had been part of Roosevelt's so-called "Brain Trust," which helped create policy for Roosevelt during the presidential election. Tugwell eventually resigned due to criticism about how he managed the RA.

The three divisions of the RA were the Land Utilization Division, the Resettlement Division, and the Rehabilitation Division. Land Utilization bought 10 million acres of land for use as parks, pastures, game preserves, or forest. The Rehabilitation Division offered training for farmers and their families, as well as administered the RA's loans. The Resettlement Division absorbed people working with the Works Progress Administration (WPA) and the Federal Emergency Relief Administration (FERA), which, in part, gave people work doing things such as building roads, planting trees, creating parks, and writing brochures and guide books.

The Plow that Broke the Plains

The RA had been looking for a filmmaker to document the economic crises that many Americans were facing. It was believed that the power of film would help generate the support needed for continued funding for the New Deal projects, especially for the controversial RA. Pare Lorentz had already proven himself as a supporter of Roosevelt and the New Deal, especially with the environmental issues in the Plains. He had already tried to get the movie industry to make a film about the Dust Bowl, but that was rejected, and he also wrote an in-depth article about the Dust Bowl for *Newsweek*. Lorentz was hired by the federal government in June 1935, despite the fact he had never made a movie before.

Lorentz's first film for the RA was a 25-minute documentary, "The Plow that Broke the Plains." The goal of the film was to raise awareness about the impact of the Dust Bowl on the farmers. With a budget of $6,000, the film cost the RA over $19,000 and Lorentz ended up paying for much of the project out of his own pocket. This may have been due, in part, to the fact that the first-time filmmaker did not keep an organized account of his expenditures and simply submitted loose receipts and notes for reimbursement. However, it may have also been due to Congress feeling that the government should not be in the movie-making business. Throughout the project there was talk that the plug would be pulled on the film, but Lorentz continued to work on it, even when it – and his $18 a day salary – were in jeopardy.

Lorentz and the film crew traveled to Colorado, Kansas, Montana, Texas, and Wyoming to get footage of the massive dust storms. He found the residents cooperative and they were especially happy to get paid for their time. Lorentz said of the people he encountered, "They still have enormous pride. We stopped some and filmed them as they went by. When we talked to them we learned much of the cruel force that has blighted them." Conflict with some of the cameramen and technical crew also plagued the project, partially because Lorentz was a movie novice and partially because many on the crew were not supporters of Roosevelt and his programs. Lorentz thought he could get around this by using stock footage from the movie studios, but they were not enthusiastic about making a propaganda film for Roosevelt and none of the studios would let Lorentz use their footage.

Lorentz did get some help from photographer Dorothea Lange, who set up a film shoot at a migrant camp in California. He was down to the end of his allotted budget by then and opted to pay someone to do the score, but he hired someone to teach him how to edit so he could edit the film himself. Lorentz felt that a powerful score was essential to accompany his footage. Ultimately, he hired Kansas native Virgil Thompson to score the film. The New York Philharmonic performed the music and on the day of the recording, Lorentz had to tell them to stop at midnight because he could not afford the overtime. Fortunately for Lorentz, the musicians agreed to keep going and finished the film score for no additional cost.

"The Plow that Broke the Plains" debuted in March 1936 at the White House. After numerous private showings, it opened to the public at the Mayflower Hotel in Washington, D.C. on May 10, 1936. In an event sponsored by the Museum of Modern Art, the film was shown with other foreign documentaries. It was a critical success, but continued to be dogged by criticism from Hollywood insiders, who said it was propaganda, not a documentary. No movie studio would send it out for commercial distribution. Lorentz personally took the film around the country and, after the owner of the Rialto Theater in New York agreed to show it, the positive response from the public led to other theaters also agreeing to screen the film. "The Plow that Broke the Plains" was just one of a series of films that Lorentz made for the government over a five year period which came to be called The Films of Merit. However, in 1940 Congress ordered that the film be taken out of circulation due to growing criticism that farming practices and not drought were blamed for the Dust Bowl.

Migrant Camps

Another area that the federal government attempted to address was the lack of adequate housing for the displaced farmers that migrated west. On one hand, those who pushed for reform thought that federal camps where places for migrants to evolve into "class-conscious agricultural laborer(s)." Most migrants did not share this view. They did not want to work for wages. They wanted to save money to buy their own land and work for themselves.

Still, many migrants relied on the federal camps to provide adequate food and shelter. The Arvin Federal Camp, nicknamed "Weedpatch" opened in 1936 in Bakersfield on land leased by the U.S. Department of Agriculture. The camp, which cost $1 per week, had a unit for the camp manager, showers, laundry facilities, toilets, tin cabins, and designated spots for tents. There was space for about 300 people and the manager was required to document who was there, if and where they were working, and any illnesses of the camp residents. Later that year, John Steinbeck, then working as a newspaper reporter, stayed near Weedpatch and interviewed migrants as part of research for "The Grapes of Wrath."

The discrimination that many of the children of the camp experienced led to them not attending school. The local schools did not want the Okies and their ill-fitting clothes and odd accents in their classrooms. Kern County Superintendent Leo Hart got calls from local residents demanding that no money be spent on these children and saying that they could not be educated. He was called a Communist and told that his job would be in jeopardy if he did not remove the Okies from public school. Still, Hart felt that the children deserved an education, so he began to meet with them in a nearby field.

With the help of the children, the Arvin Federal Emergency School was built in the field, which he leased from the government for $10. Pete Bancroft served as the principal and helped with the construction. The children grew their own food and slaughtered their own hogs, thanks to instruction from a local butcher. Their classes included math, history, aviation mechanics, and physical education. Some students learned to sew so that they could hem their own clothes and the chemistry teacher taught the girls how to make their own cosmetics. In 2003, Weedpatch was restored and continues to operate as a camp for migrant workers.

Farm Security Administration (FSA)

When the Resettlement Administration was moved to the Department of Agriculture in 1937, the FSA was developed. The FSA was responsible for providing relief funds and relocation assistance for farming families impacted by the dust, drought, and Depression. Tugwell, the head of the FSA, understood that he needed public opinion on the side of the FSA if the program was going to continue to receive funding. He convinced economist Roy Stryker, to move to Washington to head the Information Division. When Stryker asked Tugwell what he wanted from the division, Tugwell said, "Show the city people what it's like to live on the farm." The result was some of the most well known photographs of the Depression era and the Dust Bowl.

The stable of photographers that worked for Stryker includes some of the finest photographers in American history. Walker Evans, Gordon Parks, Russell Lee, Arthur Rothstein, Marion Post Wolcott, and Dorothea Lange are among the group that produced images for the FSA. In all, 164,000 negatives and 77,000 prints were made by the FSA photographers, who found a national audience for their work in newspapers and popular magazines such as *Life* and *Look*.

Another publication that received work from FSA photographers and writers was *Survey Graphic,* the companion journal to *The Survey,* created by Paul Kellogg in the early 1900s. *The Survey* covered issues that were considered progressive, such as women's suffrage, conditions in tenement housing, birth control, discrimination against immigrants and children, and the conditions in the nation's prisons. *Survey Graphic* was created for the general population, while *The Survey* was geared toward professional social workers.

Paul Taylor was an economist, professor at the University of California at Berkeley, labor expert, and, beginning in 1935, husband to Dorothea Lange. In 1939, Taylor and Lange collaborated on "American Exodus," a non-fiction account of the westward migration in the 1930s. The State Emergency Relief Association in California had hired Taylor in 1934, with the intent of documenting the conditions of the migrant workers. Every day he saw the workers in the fields of the San Joaquin Valley, which were typically Mexican or Filipino, with a few single white men mixed in with the groups of pickers. However, now he saw entire white families, many in cars with license plates from far away places such as Oklahoma and Texas, lining up for jobs.

Taylor wrote articles for *Survey Graphic,* which got the attention of another California writer, John Steinbeck. Taylor gave accounts of families moving west, hoping for something better, but finding disappointment. The migrants in Taylor's articles found work shortages, wages of less than a dollar a day, and squalid shacks. Taylor is the one who gave these migrants the label "refugees." This led to all of the people heading into the state from the Plains being lumped into the category of Dust Bowl victims, whether they were or not, but the articles were effective in bringing attention to the plight of the migrants.

However, Taylor felt that his work would have even more impact if photographs accompanied it. Lange had been doing studio photography until the Depression, which made studio work seem meaningless. In her mind, she needed to use her craft to tell the stories of how the economy was affecting ordinary people. She transformed from a studio photographer to a documentary photographer, in the mold of Jacob Riis, who had documented the deplorable conditions of the New York tenements at the turn of the century. Taylor saw her work and hired her to take photographs to go with his articles in 1934, when both were married to other people. Within a year, they would divorce their spouses and marry each other.

The work produced by Lange and Taylor showed a side to the lives of migrant field workers that was not widely known. Taylor wrote that the large landowners of the state were exploiting the workers by offering low wages and unsanitary living conditions to people who had little other choice than to accept them. Children were living in filthy tarpaper shacks with no running water, no nearby schools, no parks, and often, no food. In 1935, in response to their work, the federal government, funded two projects for public migrant housing. One was Weedpatch and the other was in Marysville, which cost the government a total of $20,000.

Migrant Mother

When Stryker saw the report, he quickly hired Lange to join his growing group of FSA photographers. On the road for weeks at a time, primarily in rural America, Lange made thousands of photos for the FSA, but one came to be the symbol of the human cost of the Dust Bowl. In February 1936, Lange was on assignment in Nipomo, California, when the FSA was still known as the Resettlement Association. After spending a month taking photographs out in the fields, she saw a sign pointing out a pea picker's camp. Lange kept driving. She just wanted to go home.

However, by the time she got 20 miles down the road, she turned around and went back, saying she was "following instinct, not reason." When she got to the camp, she approached Florence Owens Thompson, who sat in a shabby tent with her children nearby. Lange said:

> I saw and approached the hungry and desperate mother, as if drawn by a magnet. I do not remember how I explained my presence or my camera to her, but I do remember she asked me no questions. I made five exposures, working closer and closer from the same direction. I did not ask her name or her history. She told me her age, that she was thirty-two. She said that they had been living on frozen vegetables from the surrounding fields, and birds that the children killed. She had just sold the tires from her car to buy food.

Lange said that Thompson, 32 years old with seven children, seemed to understand that the photographs might help her, either directly or indirectly. When Lange returned to San Francisco, she contacted the editor of the *San Francisco News* and gave him two photographs. The editor published an article, along with the photos of Thompson, and he contacted the federal government. By the time 20,000 pounds of food arrived at the camp, Thompson and her family were gone. Many years later, Thompson said she wished the photo had never been taken, pointing out that she never received any money for it. Since Lange was working on behalf of the government and the "Migrant Mother" photo has been in the public domain since she took it, she never received royalties, either. Whether Thompson was a Dust Bowl migrant is not clear, but either way, she became the face of the Depression and yet another influence on Steinbeck as he prepared to write a novel about the Dust Bowl.

Fleeing the Dust Bowl

Another iconic image of the Dust Bowl was "Fleeing the Dust Bowl," shot by Arthur Rothstein in 1936. Rothstein was sent to Cimarron County, Oklahoma to document the effects of the Dust Bowl on the land and people. The photo shows a farmer, Arthur Coble, and his sons walking directly into the face of the wind while a building submerged by dust sits in the background. Some doubted the authenticity of the image because other photos taken that same day showed the skies were clear. Rothstein insisted there was no staging of the photograph, which was later displayed at the Metropolitan Museum of Art in New York. It should also be noted that some of the worst storms occurred when the day started off looking clear and bright.

The criticism of the image was not unusual. Many felt that the photographs intentionally portrayed the Dust Bowl victims and the migrants in an unflattering way, designed to evoke sympathy. Certainly, the point of the FSA photographers was to garner support for the New Deal programs. Those who were most opposed to public assistance, regardless of the cause, were bound to find fault with the mission of the agency. The youngest child in the shot was Darrell Coble, who was three years old at the time. Still in Oklahoma in 1977, he said, "The one that I remember come in here from the north that evening. Dad was in the field, and I don't know why as dry as it was. This thing [dust storm] rolled in there, and he got caught on the tractor… I thought maybe the world was coming to an end, I didn't know."

Chapter 4: The Dust Bowl in Popular Culture

The Grapes of Wrath

Nothing has done more to solidify an image of the Dust Bowl migrant in the minds of Americans than "The Grapes of Wrath." John Steinbeck's classic novel, published in 1939, tells of the Joad family, sharecroppers forced off of their Oklahoma farmland and into the migrant camps of California. The work is fiction, but right or wrong, many view it as a true account of a typical Dust Bowl refugee. The subject matter hit close to home for Steinbeck, a resident of California's Salinas Valley for many years. A local newspaper, the *San Francisco News,* printed several articles he wrote about migrant workers in its October 1936 edition. Photos taken by Dorothea Lange accompanied the articles. In 1938, Steinbeck published the nonfiction precursor to "The Grapes of Wrath" called "Their Blood is Strong."

Steinbeck wrote in his nonfiction pamphlet, "Our agriculture, for all its great produce, is a failure." He argued that farmers accustomed to working their own land were unable to adapt to the new, commercial farming process. He said they went from, "the old agrarian, self-containing farm where nearly everything used was raised or manufactured, to a system of agriculture so industrialized that the man who plants a crop does not often see, let alone harvest, the fruit of his planting, where the migrant has no contact with the growing cycle."

Just prior to the release of "The Grapes of Wrath," *Fortune* magazine had published an article discussing the conditions of the migrant work camps. The magazine called the situation for many of the migrants "desperate," stemming from "the whole tragic history of American agriculture, dating from the earliest misuse of soil." Through the work of Taylor and Lange, the public was already forming an impression of the migrant workers and, accurate or not, the refugees from the Dust Bowl.

Steinbeck went to Oklahoma in 1938 to do research for "The Grapes of Wrath" and discovered that many of the farmers were forced off their land by tractors, not by the Dust Bowl. Sharecroppers, who exchanged crops for rent, could not produce as quickly as machines. Steinbeck took some creative license with his novel and added in images of days darkened by dust, changed the Joad's crop from wheat to corn, and had the Joad family near the Arkansas border, out of the Dust Bowl's path. Still, the image that he created was true for those that actually did escape the Dust Bowl's wrath, making many forget that the Joads were not real. It also slapped the "Okie" label on the westward migrants and many did not like it, feeling as if they had to live it down for generations.

In 1940, director John Ford brought "The Grapes of Wrath" to the silver screen with Henry Fonda playing the role of Tom Joad. The screenplay differs from the novel, placing the Joad family in a government-run migrant camp, leading up to a happier ending than the novel. The politics are also dulled down, including the elimination of references to socialism and "the reds." Interestingly, the movie never actually shows any of the characters working in the fields, but it still went a long way toward solidifying America's image of migrants from the Plains and the ravages of the Dust Bowl. In 1989, the Library of Congress selected the movie, which won an Academy Award for Ford and for Jane Darwell, who played Ma Joad, as one of the most historically significant films in history and marked it as one of the first 25 films to be preserved in the United States National Film Treasury.

Bruce Springsteen revived the image of Tom Joad in his 1995 album, "The Ghost of Tom Joad." Springsteen said it was the movie that inspired the album about the difficulties of life in America and Mexico in the mid-1990s. Lyrics of the title track include the verse, "Men walkin' 'long the railroad tracks, Goin' someplace, there's no goin' back. Highway patrol choppers comin' up over the ridge — Hot soup on a campfire under the bridge," which is an obvious reference to the migrants. The song was inspired by Woody Guthrie's folk ballad, "The Ballad of Tom Joad."

Woody Guthrie

Some have labeled folk singer Woody Guthrie the Dust Bowl poet, although his body of work encompassed more than ballads about the Dust Bowl refugees. Reviled by some for his left-leaning political views, Guthrie's work served as the voice for many of the poor and disenfranchised during the Great Depression. He was in Southern California during the Depression and got a first-hand look at the migrant camps and heard accounts of how the dust and drought had driven some farm families from the their land. It was something he was already familiar with, coming from Pampa, Texas. He channeled some of what he saw and heard into the only record he ever cut for a major record label, Dust Bowl Ballads, released by RCA in 1940.

Tracks on Dust Bowl Ballads include, "Dust Pneumonia Blues," "Dust Bowl Blues" and "Tom Joad," a song in two parts that was inspired by "The Grapes of Wrath." Guthrie notes the blockades set up at the California borders to keep out the poor with "Do-Re-Mi." He sings, "California is a garden of Eden, a paradise to live in or to see, but believe it or not, you won't find it so hot, if you ain't got the do-re-mi." The Library of Congress Recordings of the album is a three-record set, put on vinyl for a radio show at a government-owned station in 1940. There are 28 songs, as well as an interview with Alan Lomax, folklorist and musicologist for the Library of Congress, and Elizabeth Littleton, Lomax's wife.

Guthrie did some work directly for the federal government during the Depression. In 1941, he accepted a month-long assignment with the Bonneville Power Administration, which was one of Roosevelt's New Deal projects. The government wanted songs about the dams that were being constructed near the Columbia River in the Pacific Northwest. Guthrie wrote 26 songs in 30 days including the official state folk song of Washington, "Roll on, Columbia."

Guthrie was also an author of the semi-fictional "Bound for Glory" and "Seeds of Man," but his novel about the Dust Bowl was undiscovered until recently. "House of Earth" will be edited by author Douglas Brinkley and actor Johnny Depp and is due to be released in 2013. In December 1936, Guthrie was in New Mexico working as a street performer, fleeing the dust of Texas. In New Mexico, Guthrie was fascinated with the sturdy adobe houses, built of simple materials but far more structurally sound than the cheap wood-framed houses he saw in Texas. After spending five cents on a pamphlet from the U.S. Department of Agriculture on how to build adobe structures and use them on farmland, Guthrie became convinced that this was what the farmers hit by the Dust Bowl needed to withstand the harsh elements of the Plains.

Back in Pampa in the late 1930s, Guthrie wrote to his friend, actor Eddie Albert, telling him of the sleet that had mixed with dust, turning the sleet the color of "cocoa." *The New York Times* described it as "a blizzard of frozen mud." Guthrie wrote, "Well Howdy. We didn't have no trouble finding the dust bowl, and are about as covered up as one family can get. Only trouble is the dust is so froze up it cain't blow, so it just scrapes around." He dreamed of having an adobe hacienda, like the ones he saw in New Mexico, to offer more protection to his family from the harsh winter weather. "You dig you a cellar and mix the mud and straw right in there, sorta with your feet, you know, and you get the mud just the right thickness, and you put in a mould, and you mould out around 20 bricks a day and in a reasonable length of time you have got enough to build your house."

When Lomax read the first chapter of "House of Earth," which tells off the struggles of a young Texas couple, living on land where adobe houses are forbidden, he encouraged Guthrie to get it published. Guthrie did finish the manuscript in 1947, but did nothing more with it after that, perhaps sensing the changing political tides as the U.S. entered into the Cold War era. The graphic sex scenes may have also been a barrier to getting it published, as was Guthrie's use of downhome, Plains dialect. One person who did like it was Bob Dylan, who was "surprised by the genius" of the work. Before Guthrie could revisit the idea of publishing his novel, he became sick from Huntington's Disease, which eventually took his life.

Chapter 5: Long-Term Effects of the Dust Bowl

The drought needed in 1941 when the Plains were soaked with drenching rains. It is difficult to determine the direct costs of the Dust Bowl because it is enmeshed with the Great Depression. The economy then experienced a sharp recovery with the start of World War II. However, it is estimated that over one billion dollars from the federal government were spent on drought-related conditions in the 1930s. The biggest economic downfall from the Dust Bowl was the cost of migration. Thousands of people left the region and while many returned, many did not. It also resulted in depressed wages in the areas where the migrant pickers eventually found work.

The AAA subsidy system has continued, as has the Soil Conservation Service, now named the Natural Resources Conservation Service. Certainly, more attention is given to sustainable agricultural and soil management practices. However, land use in the 1940s changed very little. Farmers were slow to admit that they had any hand in creating the Dust Bowl and were not eager to change their practices – some never did. Some implemented new procedures such as contour plowing, which is plowing rows that follow the natural curve of the land as opposed to going directing up and over the slopes, which can create channels that carry away topsoil or seed. Contour plowing slows the flow of water and saves the topsoil by creating ridges. Terrace plowing is similar in that furrows go up mountainous regions in patterns that look like stair steps.

Economically, the Dust Bowl is proven to have reduced land values in the short and long term. The cost in the 1930s is estimated to have been $153 million and adjusted for today, the cost would be closer to $2 billion. Areas of the Dust Bowl with the highest soil erosion found that their costs to produce crops, or revenue per acre, rose and some never completely recovered. It is difficult to extract how much of that was related to the Depression and not, specifically, the Dust Bowl.

Throughout the Depression and into the 1950s, land was not reallocated to activities that would be considered more productive, such as using it for livestock. Even into the latter stages of the 20th century, the same amount of land was devoted to crops as had been used in the first half of the century. The primary difference was that as time went on, the farms became bigger and the small family farm was less prevalent. Very little cropland converted back into pastures. The threat of dust storms is still existent and environmental scientists warn that unless there is a major reform in farming techniques, the threat of another Dust Bowl remains.

Conclusion

The impact of the Dust Bowl changed the United States forever. It literally altered the landscape, as well as the way man interacts with land and nature. The mass migration changed the state of California, too, as the people of the Plains brought their own set of values and customs, as well as their work ethic. Even though many that left the Plains eventually returned, many set roots in California and started new lives for their families. Perhaps nothing changed as much as the federal government, which was faced with acknowledging its own role in creating the dust storms, and then faced with persuading the nation that it was the government's role to help solve the problems. Despite the critics of Roosevelt's New Deal, no doubt many Americans would not have survived with the government aid. In time, as generations have passed, it has become accepted that the farmers unwittingly played a role in the great disaster. However, they have also left behind lessons that can help today's farmers and growers avoid a similar ecological disaster.

Made in the USA
San Bernardino, CA
22 April 2013